.97

The Great Dilemma
of World Organization

The Great Dilemma
of World Organization

By FREMONT RIDER

WESLEYAN UNIVERSITY, MIDDLETOWN, CONN.

REYNAL & HITCHCOCK

NEW YORK CITY

To Ruth

CONTENTS

The author takes this opportunity to express his appreciation of constructive criticism received from several of his faculty colleagues, especially from Professors Samuel H. Brockunier, Alexander Cowie and Alan B. Overstreet. Also from the statistical division of the United States Office of Education.

I. THE DILEMMA

A T THIS moment in its history the world is facing, with an uneasy lack of confidence, a Great Dilemma to which it can see no satisfactory solution. It wants to set up a world organization that will really assure permanent peace, and the Dilemma prevents its doing so.

"*Wants* to set up?" Haven't we just finished the organization of a new league of nations? Yes, we have. But let us look at the history of this last year quite dispassionately. It is true that we have set up, with many speeches and much newspaper publicity, a new United Nations Organization. But where, in any direction whatsoever, as I write this sentence in March 1946, can I see any one of the great powers taking its "assurance" of peace seriously? Have we, here in the United States, because of its establishment, cut down one whit on our military strength? On the contrary, we have planned, "because of new post-war obligations", a quintupling in size of our pre-war regular army; are drafting plans for $100,000,000 even bigger (but already obsolete) battleships; and are busily planning the securing and the development of (already outmoded) naval bases all over the world. Have Great Britain or France or Holland taken the new league any more into account than we have in the formulation of their national policies? On the contrary, by every art of diplomacy, by aggressive or defensive action on every economic front, and by not a little actual fighting, they have, all through this past year, been struggling, with pitifully depleted resources, to rebuild their shattered national empires and protect them against the fresh encroachments that they fear. As for Russia, the most frightened, or the most ambitious, of all the nations—analyze her acts either way, as you please—has she not, in those acts, and in what very little we know of her plans, ignored almost contemptuously both the ideals and the precepts of the new league? She certainly has been ruthless and tireless in a thousand directions in the expansion of her national boundaries and "spheres of influence" and in the increasing of the fundamentals of her power to wage war. She even announces quite frankly that this last is definitely her first policy.

In other words, if we were going to appraise honestly the impact of our new league of nations on the world's military and political reshufflings, we would have to say that it, like its predecessor league that failed so dismally, has so far been treated as merely another piece to be moved about on the international board in the game for national power— and as a not very important piece at that. We would have to say that the great nations treat it as a popularly appealing "front," as something to talk about approvingly. But, as something to rely on, instead of one's own armies, for one's own protection; as something actually to take into account when one is formulating one's own national policies—well, one

ought not to be ridiculous! Yet the peoples of the
world desperately want a world organization for peace
that is *not* thus impotent. They want a world order
that will *stop* the United States from further increasing
its military power, one that will *stop* Great Britain
and France from the exercise of further nationalistic
ambitions, one that will *stop* Russia's further "infil-
trations" and attempts to gain either military or political or economic control of her neighbor states. And
they want a world order that will stop all things of
this sort, not primarily through the exercise of its own
arbitrary military power, but mainly because every
one of the great powers will realize that, in the new
order, no act of these kinds that each is now so busy
with is any longer necessary for its national safety
and well being. *That* is the sort of a world organization that the peoples of the world are asking for—and
are not now getting. What then is this Great Dilemma
that stands in the way of their getting it?

There is nothing esoteric about it. It derives directly
from three unescapable sets of facts. The first one is
that, since all nations of the world are now "sovereign," it is necessary for them—if they are going to
form a real world-state—to agree among themselves,
in advance, as to what share of power in that world-
state each one of them is going to have. The second
fact is that these sovereign states vary enormously in
their sizes, populations, and military and economic
powers. The third fact is that the uncivilized folk of
the world overwhelmingly outnumber its civilized folk,
and so would, if they were given individual votes in
a world state, out-vote them.

Each one of these three parts of the Dilemma is, of itself, puzzling enough; but each is made still more difficult to resolve by the unfortunate additional fact that the division of the world's peoples between "civilized" and "uncivilized" happens to coincide, to a large degree, with both national and racial boundary lines. If only all the ignorant and unkempt and half-starved peoples of the world were distributed evenly among all of its countries and all of its races, there would be plenty of unpleasant problems for each one of these countries and races to solve, but not the gratuitous complication of segregated backwardness to block the setting up of a world-state. For it is because we have enormous compact masses of red and black and yellow peoples, who have been so long held down by historical and economic and religious circumstance as to have created vast areas of potential political dynamite, that the civilized peoples of the world look with trepidation at any proposal to include them in a world-state on equal terms. If world power were to be exercised on a simple population basis, Europe, for example, sees that it would be out-voted by India alone—disease-threatened, caste-ridden, economically weak India. And it is not at all unnatural that it should recoil from this prospect.

But these same differences in national cultural development, these same questions as to the distribution of national power in a world-state, present themselves, even if not so obviously, in each of the separate continents. Take Europe. Sweden and Bulgaria are substantially equal in population: would they agree that they are substantially equal in world importance?

Would the rest of us agree that these two countries are, at present, substantially equal in what they have to contribute to world governance? Or, to go directly to the heart of the problem, to the question of relative power in the world-state in its most acute and most puzzling aspects, what is going to be the voting strength in it of the four or five greatest powers? Take France—strong culturally but weak militarily: she has for a year or more been piqued because she has not been one of the "Big Three". Take Russia, struggling frantically to become quickly the world's dominant military power: what relative world-state ranking would she be satisfied with? Take ourselves in the United States, at the present moment, by common consent, the most powerful nation on earth, the wealthiest, the one possessing still the maximum of personal liberty, the one to which all other nations turn hopefully for help. Would our own people ever consent, just because three or four other countries are greater than we are in population, to yield to them voting superiority in a world-state? And would the world as a whole really want us to do so?

And yet—and this in essence is the Dilemma—if we are to have a united world order of free men and women everywhere what measuring-stick for voting power in it other than population can we take? If we are going to pay anything more than hypocritical lip-service to democracy, what logical reason could we give if India did make half-wistful, half-bitter demand for voting power in it equal to her numbers? What answer could we give to Russia, if, on the basis of population, she demanded a voting power in it far greater than our own? It is such intensely practical and immediate questions as these that constitute the problem that has so far effectually estopped the setting up of a really effective world organization. We have so far been utterly unable to devise any sort of formula for national representation in it that will accomplish two things: that will first, satisfy national prides and prestiges by truly reflecting each nation's real importance in the world, and that will, second, quiet the fears, for their future, of the civilized peoples of the world, and satisfy the aspirations, for *their* future, of the uncivilized and half-civilized ones.

Now, every would-be planner of world organization is well aware of the existence of this Dilemma. Also he knows in his heart that it is the crux of the practicality of his plan. But, just because it has always seemed an almost insoluble problem, each planner has either ignored it entirely, or has "solved" it only in terms of more or less vague generalities. Take, for example, Mr. Emery Reves' "The Anatomy of Peace", which has received much comment lately. Perhaps it is unfair to call this book a "plan" at all, for it is rather an appeal for a world-state than a definite proposal for one, an appeal making up in apostolic fervor what it lacks in definiteness. What is its solution for the Great Dilemma? So far as its author gives one it appears in the following sentences in his two concluding paragraphs: "We shall have to organize peace independently of the Unholy Alliance still born in San Francisco . . . or else we shall delude ourselves . . . until the inevitable march of

events into another and greater holocaust teaches us
that equal and sovereign power units can never . . .
co-exist peacefully . . . After a disastrous half a century of antirationalism . . . we must return to ration-
alism . . . The task is by no means easy . . . There
is no other fate for us than to climb the long, hard,
steep, and stony road guided by . . . reason."

The trouble with this sort of thing is that it doesn't
get us anywhere. Little appeal needs to be made for
the world-state as a theory: in the abstract almost
every one is already in favor of it. It is the world-
state in whatever concrete form it has so far been
put that has failed to win adherents. Yet, until it has
been put into concrete form, has been made a definite proposal, all argument in favor of it is bound
to be more or less *words*. The peoples of the world
are demanding, not vague generalities, but an extremely definite, and profoundly reasonable, answer
to this question: "what exactly is to be the voting
power of each of the nations in your world organization, and by what formula is this voting power ar-
rived at?" Until they get such an answer they are
not going to give up their national powers to any
new order whatsoever, no matter how persuasive the
arguments in favor of their doing so may seem to be.

And this brings us face to face with another fact
about which also we ought to stop trying to fool ourselves. If *any* world organization is going to fulfill
its purpose, it will be absolutely necessary for us to
give up to it some of the most important of our
national powers. What we Americans have really
wanted has been to have a league of nations to keep

all the other nations of the world at peace, and at the same time to keep ourselves strong enough militarily to resist possible aggression from any quarter. In other words, we didn't really trust our league, and wanted a sort of double insurance. This would have been fine except for one thing: every other great power felt just the same way that we did, and wanted just exactly this same sort of double insurance. The inevitable result has been that our two insurances have cancelled each other out and have left us all without any insurance whatever.

At the present moment it isn't good form to say out loud that our newly set up United Nations Organization isn't working as it was intended to. We are told that the second session in London went off pretty well. From some standpoints it did. At least the new league didn't blow up before it was born. The very fact that it was born was something. People talked freely: that was all to the good too. Nevertheless, what, specifically and concretely, did this session accomplish to reduce present armaments, to remove immediately annoying national frictions, to stop now existing great power aggressions on weak neighbors, to bring genuine world peace any nearer? The answer has to be: disappointingly little. Maybe it is a wise policy to utter brave words about the "successful" first meeting of the U. N. O. and deliberately to shut our eyes to a great many unpleasant facts. But not all of us are content to do this.

As a matter of fact, scores of individuals, in every walk of life and in every country, have felt from the start that no league *of nations* was ever going to accomplish much. Take Hutchins, of the University of Chicago: "It may be that the atomic bomb is the 'good news of damnation', that will . . . frighten us into . . . the creation of a world society, not a thousand . . . years hence, but now." Take Bolté, chairman of the American Veterans Committee: "The atomic age demands a new pattern of inter-national . . . relations: . . . an end to the unbridled sovereignty of nations." Take Einstein: "The secret of the bomb should be committed to a *world government* . . . to it all nations should commit all their military strength." Now it is easy to dismiss these quotations, and hundreds of others that could be made like them, by saying that they come from "dreamers" and "idealists", though Bolté is a war veteran, and college presidents are not exactly dreamers. But can this form of dismissal be applied to the significant statement made by Mr. Ernest Bevin in the House of Commons on November 23d last? "I am willing to sit with anybody, of any party, of any nation, to try to devise a franchise or a constitution . . . for a World Assembly . . . with a limited objective—the objective of peace . . . a world law with a world judiciary to interpret it, with a world police to enforce it, with the decision of the people with their own votes resting in their own hands, irrespective of race or creed, as the great world sovereign elected authority which would hold in its care the destinies of the people of the world."

All this does not mean that the present writer—unlike Reves and some other world-state advocates—disapproves of our present league of nations and what it is trying to do. On the contrary he wishes it well. He very earnestly hopes to see it grow in power, and importance. It even seems to him barely —just barely—possible that, despite all our fears to the contrary, it may surprise us all by accomplishing what it was set up to accomplish.

But, in the meantime, two things seem to him vitally desirable: first, that we do not shut our eyes to present facts, that we see clearly the things that are really transpiring in the world and take note that they are not the things that we wish were happening there. If we stick our heads in the sand there is grave danger that the United Nations Organization will lull us into a fatally false security. Second, it would seem that we ought, all the while, whether our new league of nations is going ill or well, to study the possibilities of achieving a real world-state. For, if things go ill with our league of nations, and it fails us, we shall *have* to come to a world-state, and perhaps come to it very quickly indeed in the face of immediately impending, world-wide disaster. To be prepared to meet such a possible crisis would seem to be taking out the irreducible minimum of insurance. If, on the contrary, things go well with our new league they make a possible world-state just that much more practicable, for they pave the way for it and make it easier to bring it about. But in that case also we ought meanwhile to be preparing some sort of a plan for it, even though in this case it be a plan to meet not a crisis but an opportunity.

Why do we assume that no league *of nations* is likely to accomplish for us what the occasion demands? Because, so long as we continue to have politically "sovereign" nations, we continue to have national fears, rivalries, hatreds, prides, and ambitions. Having them, every nation thinks it necessary to have national military power to defend itself. And, having military power, every nation, sooner or later, gets into a war with some other nation. That, in all the world's past history, has been the inevitable chain of sequence. If there is any argument in precedent there is every reason to believe that we shall never be able to get completely away from war until we are able to get completely away from nationality *in inter-national affairs.* On the other hand, no nation—none of us—is going to be willing to give up its own military protections, however fearful we may be of their adequacy, until we are convinced of the permanent soundness, of the innate and unshakable equitableness, of the proposed new order. Which, of course, brings us back to the original Dilemma. And makes it the vitally—indeed the overwhelmingly—important problem that it is.

We said above "to avoid immediate and world-wide disaster". Whatever our statesmen may think, the plain peoples of the world don't need to be told that the Dilemma is not a problem whose solution can be indefinitely evaded or postponed. They saw, even as our new league of nations was being born, a relatively small bomb dropped on a relatively unknown Japanese city named Hiroshima. Hiroshima went up in smoke; and, when it did, what little confidence they had been able to work up in the just-being-refurbished league-of-nations went up in smoke too. Thereafter we might all continue to cry "Peace!" "Peace!" as loudly as ever; but in our hearts we knew that it was no longer to be bought at so small a price. The atomic bomb in August didn't change the text of a single one of the international agreements which we had just signed in April. It did something far more disconcerting than that. It forced us to look at what we had all been trying not to see: namely that no agreements between sovereign *nations* to do something, or not to do something, are likely ever to amount to much. Of this sad fact we had been amply warned. We had seen, during the very decade just past, the national "honor" backing up such agreements reach an all-time low. Never, in all history, were treaties between sovereign states entered into more cynically, or breached more casually, than now, in our own time. Furthermore, right up to the moment I write we are continuing to be warned. Every day since last April the thing has been going right on. Every day, with the ink still wet on our very latest international agreements, we watch them being breached daily by double-talk and indirection and outright disregard. And yet—even yet, until Hiroshima—we continued to *hope*. Since Hiroshima, we have begun to see the fallacy of hoping, and have at last begun to demand something more.

We just said "we." Exactly who are this "we" that we are talking about? It might be well to look at ourselves for a moment—as a whole. "We" are two billion or more human beings, of all sorts of languages, colors, creeds and degrees of civilization, living on the skin of a ball twenty-five thousand miles around. Different though we are in many things, the overwhelming majority of us agree on one thing: we desire to live at peace with our neighbors. All through history the majority of us have abhorred war and have lived in the constant fear of it. But, very recently indeed, this fear has pressed on us all with redoubled force because of two facts which are entirely new in history; first, that we are now able to reach any spot on the skin of our ball, from any other spot on it, in less than two days, and, second, that—this probably will be a fact in the next year or two—the most highly populated spots on the ball will be within rocket-bomb reach of each other in a few minutes.

"We" are, at present, governed by something over seventy different "national" sovereignties, ranging in size from Vatican City's one thousand inhabitants to China's four hundred and eighty million. Some of these sovereignties, like the British Commonwealth, the United States, and the Union of Soviet Socialist Republics, are in turn themselves leagues of "sovereignties", and some of these sub-sovereignties are greater in population than most of the completely independent nations.

Because, as we have said, most of the wars of history—including practically all of those in the last three centuries—have been the result of either nationalistic fears or nationalistic ambitions, we have sought to prevent them by trying to curb nationalism. That is all any league of nations is, a device to put restraints on nationalistic power. Not much restraint; for, in leagues of nations the nations leagued insist upon retaining all the power they have always had to do exactly as they please; the only restraint is that, in certain directions, they agree with each other not to use it. But the fact we have already noted, that agreements of this sort between nations, although they have been made thousands of times in the past, have always been ignored just as soon as national interest dictated, makes our faith in the efficacy of all league-of-nation agreements a very shaky faith indeed.

The second possible form of world political organization, one not of armed sovereign nations but of one single World-State of individuals, is something that political idealists have talked about for centuries. Leagues of nations have been tried out scores of times: they have always failed to maintain peace. Maybe the World-State would fail too: we don't know: it has never been tried. To all of the world's more thoughtful men and women, however, the dream of securing political world unity has always made strong appeal. For the more sensitive a man's understanding is the more repugnant the ugly realities of crime, war, and intolerance are. Artists, musicians, writers and such folk have always looked upon all the peoples of the world as their audience, and scientists and engineers have had little use for national boundaries.

As a matter of fact, probably most of those who, in these past years, have been working for world peace through our two leagues of nations have done so mainly for reasons of expediency. If asked, they would admit that they were not taking the logical, or even the most promising, road to peace. They would probably admit that they were hoping from the new

United Nations Organization little more than that it might be able to avoid the more obvious of those errors of spirit and procedure that dogged the steps of its predecessor league. And it wouldn't make much difference If they tried to deny their doubts of its basic instability, for these doubts have cropped up continually. They cropped up, for example, in the very phraseology which its organizers used when they were formulating the United Nations charter. Such phrases as "putting teeth" into things, and "delimiting possible areas of conflict," etc., etc., are, after all, the phrases of truce, not the phrases describing any assured and enduring peace. This statement isn't intended to imply that the architects of the new United Nations Organization have been insincere. Rather they have been acting on the theory that a half-loaf is better than none; that, if the world is not yet ready to build a world organization fashioned politically as perfectly as may be, it is the part of wisdom now to build the best substitute we can.

II. PREVIOUS ATTEMPTS TO SOLVE THE DILEMMA

I N ORDER that we may have the Great Dilemma very clearly in our minds as we go on, it may be well for us at this point to take a sort of bird's eye view of the populations of each of the various nations of the world, with some indication of their respective racial make-ups.*

*In Table "A" following, "Non-White" means Mongolian, Negro, American Indian, Malayan, etc. (including all mixed populations.)

TABLE A.

Estimated Population of the Countries of the World, By Races

These are the latest published figures (of various dates) with estimated adjustments to bring them up to date, and in some cases with estimated adjustments to special post-war situations. In nearly all cases figures are given only to the nearest even million. "Min." means "probably less than one million."

	White	Non-White	Total
United States	125,000,000	15,000,000	140,000,000
Russia	178,000,000	10,000,000	188,000,000
England & Wales	42,000,000	Min.	42,000,000
Scotland	5,000,000	Min.	5,000,000
Ireland	3,000,000	Min.	3,000,000
British India	Min.	396,000,000	396,000,000
Australia	7,300,000	Min.	7,300,000
New Zealand	1,700,000	Min.	1,700,000
South Africa	2,000,000	8,000,000	10,000,000
Canada	11,000,000	Min.	12,000,000
Burma	Min.	15,000,000	15,000,000
Other British Colonies	2,000,000	72,000,000	74,000,000
Total for British Empire	74,000,000	492,000,000	566,000,000

	White	Non-White	Total
China	Min.	480,000,000	480,000,000
Holland	9,000,000	Min.	9,000,000
Dutch Indonesia	Min.	68,000,000	68,000,000
Italy	46,000,000	Min.	46,000,000
France	38,000,000	Min.	38,000,000
Algeria	1,000,000	7,000,000	8,000,000
French Indo China	Min.	24,000,000	24,000,000
French Morocco	Min.	7,000,000	7,000,000
Tunisia	Min.	3,000,000	3,000,000
Other French Colonies	Min.	55,000,000	55,000,000
Total French Empire	39,000,000	96,000,000	135,000,000
Portugal and Portuguese Colonies	8,000,000	7,000,000	15,000,000
Germany	70,000,000	Min.	70,000,000
Belgium and Belgian Colonies	8,000,000	10,000,000	18,000,000
Spain and Spanish Colonies	26,000,000	3,000,000	29,000,000
Luxembourg	Min.	Min.	Min.
Switzerland	4,300,000	Min.	4,300,000
Denmark	3,900,000	Min.	3,900,000
Norway	2,900,000	Min.	2,900,000
Sweden	6,600,000	Min.	6,600,000
Finland	3,800,000	Min.	3,800,000
Latvia	1,600,000	Min.	1,600,000

Estonia	1,000,000	Min.	1,000,000
Lithuania	2,700,000	Min.	2,700,000
Poland	28,000,000	Min.	28,000,000
Czechoslovakia	10,000,000	Min.	10,000,000
Austria	5,800,000	Min.	5,800,000
Hungary	13,000,000	Min.	13,000,000
Rumania	9,000,000	Min.	9,000,000
Bulgaria	6,600,000	Min.	6,600,000
Albania	Min.	Min.	Min.
Greece	6,000,000	Min.	6,000,000
Jugoslavia	15,000,000	Min.	15,000,000
Japan	Min.	72,000,000	72,000,000
Korea	Min.	23,000,000	23,000,000
Philippines	Min.	16,000,000	16,000,000
Siam	Min.	15,000,000	15,000,000
Afghanistan	Min.	12,000,000	12,000,000
Persia	Min.	14,000,000	14,000,000
Iraq	Min.	5,000,000	5,000,000
Arabia	Min.	5,000,000	5,000,000
Turkey	Min.	17,000,000	17,000,000
Syria & Lebanon	Min.	4,000,000	4,000,000
Egypt	Min.	16,000,000	16,00,000
Ethiopia	Min.	12,000,000	12,000,000
Liberia	Min.	1,500,000	1,500,000
Brazil	16,000,000	26,000,000	42,000,000

	White	Non-White	Total
Argentina	13,000,000	1,000,000	14,000,000
Chile	4,000,000	1,000,000	5,000,000
Uruguay	Min.	1,500,000	2,000,000
Paraguay	Min.	Min.	1,000,000
Bolivia	Min.	2,600,000	3,000,000
Ecuador	Min.	2,000,000	3,000,000
Peru	Min.	4,000,000	6,000,000
Colombia	3,000,000	6,000,000	9,000,000
Venezuela	Min.	3,000,000	4,000,000
Panama	Min.	Min.	600,000
Costa Rica	Min.	Min.	600,000
Guatemala	Min.	3,200,000	3,500,000
Honduras	Min.	Min.	1,000,000
Salvador	Min.	2,000,000	2,200,000
Nicaragua	Min.	900,000	1,000,000
Cuba	3,200,000	1,200,000	4,400,000
Haiti	Min.	3,000,000	3,000,000
Dominican Republic	Min.	1,700,000	1,700,000
Mexico	3,000,000	17,000,000	20,000,000
Other parts of world	Min.	12,000,000	12,000,000
TOTALS	745,400,000	1,481,600,000	2,235,700,000

So far we have referred to the Dilemma as though it were a problem that presented itself only to would-be planners of world-states. Of course, this isn't true at all. Every league-of-nations has to face it, too. But leagues-of-nations have to face it from a different angle, and from an angle from which it is easier to evade it. It was remarked in the previous chapter that cultural "backwardness" tends to coincide with national boundary lines. And the reason that the Dilemma is a problem for leagues-of-nations, as well as for world-states, is that the backward peoples of the world as nations, are, like the backward peoples of the world as individuals, in a voting majority. It is, nevertheless, because leagues-of-nations face the Dilemma in its national form that they find it easier to evade it. As nations, they are under no obligation to make even a pretense of "democratic" equality. The big nations need not try very hard to hide the fact that they intend to hold the reins tight over their lesser, or backward, sister nations.

So in leagues-of-nations, although it has been deemed politic to cloak this domination a little in some way, the evasive formula used for the "solution" of the Dilemma is a very transparent one indeed. Look over all the proposals which have been made for such leagues—and a recent study summarized briefly no less than twenty-eight of them! Not a single one of them comes out flatly and says that, because "X" state is two (or ten, or a hundred) times more powerful militarily, or more wealthy, or more populous, than "Y" state, it ought, in the proposed league, to have two (or ten, or a hundred) times as much voting power. To *that* extent the league-of-nations planners try to save national "face". Nevertheless they see to it that the big-state members of their league control it.

There are various methods. The "solution" adopted by the first League of Nations was an "Assembly" of fifty-five nations, in which Assembly each nation had a single vote. But this Assembly was really but little more than a debating society, because over it was imposed a "Council" of fourteen members, in which five of the great powers—France, Germany, Great Britain, Italy and Japan—had "permanent" seats. The new United Nations Organization follows almost exactly this same pattern: it too has an equal-vote "Assembly" of the fifty-one nations so far admitted to its membership, but this time the super-imposed "Council"—now given the more persuasive name of "Security Council"—concentrates control even more certainly in the militarily great powers, for it has only six small-nation members instead of the first League's nine. The five "permanent" Council members this time are the United States, Great Britain, Russia, China and France; and, whereas, in the League of Nations, it was the United States (always) and Russia (at the end) which were not members, this time it is the "Axis" powers which are left outside the fold. In the two decades between the founding of the two leagues of nations one important realization has, however, developed among the smaller nations of the world; and has been accepted by them as a fact that— willy-nilly—has to be accepted: namely that the peace of the world actually does hang upon the acts and policies of its three or four greatest powers, and any league of nations plan must be developed around this fact.

This particular method of maintaining great-nation control of a league-of-nations, i.e. by a self-selected "Council" super-imposed over an Assembly of all the nations, is the only one that has—within recent years—had actual trial. But various other methods have been suggested. Several league-of-nation planners have developed one form or another of the regional-group, or area-group, idea. Mr. Eli Culbertson, for example, ingeniously proposed, first to divide the world into eleven "regional federations" (viz. American, British, Latin-European, Germanic, Middle Eastern, Russian, Chinese, Japanese, Malaysian and Indian), and then to group these eleven regional federations into a world federation. He frankly admitted that his plan was based on no principle but the pragmatic one of being, it seemed to him, the one most likely to overcome national resistance to the plan. Other planners have, instead, proposed "continental" regions. Still others "hemispheric" regions. Still others "racial" regions.

On quite a different basis—on what we might, perhaps, term the "exclusive-club" idea—has rested another much publicized plan, Mr. Clarence K. Streit's "Union Now." This plan proposed a "federal union" of the "leading democracies," beginning first with the United States and the British Commonwealth. This initial grouping was, according to its proposer, to be followed by "a more general type of world organization", which was to be composed of "this union of democracies, the Union of Soviet Socialist Republics, China, and the other members of the United Nations." You will note that it was to be "followed": it was felt by its planner that "full federal union" with such a nation as

Russia, for example, was not "practically attainable at present." Like Mr. Culbertson's plan, Mr. Streit's was worked out in considerable detail, and was an appealing one in many respects. Unfortunately, however, as critics of it at once pointed out, its immediate tendency would be to divide the world, at the start, into three sets of two groups each. There would be one division of the nations of the world into two groups having opposing economic and political ideologies. At the same time the plan divided the world between the "haves" and the "have nots", and between its uncivilized peoples and its civilized. Obviously any one of these three kinds of world division had within it the seeds of world war: all three kinds together were almost sure to render assured peace unobtainable.

This Streit idea of starting a world-state piece-meal, beginning with any two or three nations who might "want to come in", and then growing, is an intriguing one. But it would seem to be a practicable one only if we have, from the start, a very definite plan, a plan with a place in it, on equal terms, for every country that may later want to come in. We can never have real world health if our plan permits the economic and social cancer spots of the world to remain indefinitely cancerous. Our "solution" for the Dilemma, whatever it is, must be one that attacks at once, and works strongly to cure, the cancers. It must, in other words, be one that not only includes, from the start, the world's backward peoples, but includes them in such a way as gives them a definite means, a definite desire, and a definite reward, to improve their political and economic status. It must, in short, be a plan that will inspire them to become more "civilized", meaning by "civilized" better prepared to take—if not at once, at least in due course—their proportionate share of world responsibility.

If now we turn from league-of-nation plans and look at world-state ones, we find just one—or at least I have been able to find just one—that offered any *definite* solution at all for the Dilemma. This was the plan presented by Professor Bordwell, Dean of the Law School of the University of Iowa. He very persuasively disarmed criticism—American criticism at least—by taking the Constitution of the United States, and, with relatively few changes, making it fit the needs of his proposed world-state. But exactly how did he propose to meet the Dilemma? His solution for it is to be found in the fine print of Section 3 of Article I of his Constitution. It says that the number of members of the world "Assembly . . . shall not exceed one for every 2,500,000 . . . inhabitants, but no nation shall have more than ten or less than one member." Now this formula is definite enough. But how "practical" is it? That is, how far would it go towards securing a vote of approval from either the legislators, or the peoples, of any one of the world's great powers? And how well would the world be governed under the set-up that it proposes? Under it, as we can see by examining "Table A." the United States and Great Britain and Russia would be cut down to a parity in voting power with such countries as India, Korea, Brazil, Poland, Japan, Spain, and Indonesia. Would *you* vote for such a distribution as this of voting power in a world-state to which you were asked to surrender your nation's entire military strength?

There is one other, and quite different, basis for distributing national voting power in a world-state, which has cropped up in a number of places. Ex-Governor Harold Stassen, for instance, mentioned it in an address before the Foreign Policy Association. He proposed—to quote his exact words—that, in "a continuing organization of the United Nations of the World", of which the "key governmental device" was to be "a single-house parliament", "representation and voting power" should be "based upon a formula which would take into consideration the numbers of the literate population of the respective nations . . . and the resources of the member nations." Here we have the new basis (that is a basis other than population)—"resources".

At Dublin, N. H. last October some fifty men and women, leaders in the crusade for world peace, who had met to discuss the political implications of the harnessing of atomic energy, after several days of discussion gave (somewhat qualified) assent to a plan for a world-state *of peoples,* with very limited but very definite powers. And they also proposed that representation in this state was to be based on "natural and industrial resources". To be sure, to "resources", they added "population and other relevant factors". As to what the "other relevant factors" were to be they said nothing whatever, and even as to "resources" they were disappointingly vague.

And that is the trouble with "national resources" as a possible measuring stick of voting power: the idea sounds plausible until we analyze it and try to pin it down into concrete terms. Then we become tangled up in a number of very puzzling subsidiary questions.

In the first place, what sorts of resources shall we select? Shall we take "natural" ones only, like oil and coal and copper and iron ore? These are hidden in the ground: we can measure them by estimate, but, almost surely, some of the greatest of them we are at this moment unaware even of the existence of. Yet difficulties of measurement would be the least of our troubles. There are political difficulties. If we select "natural resources" only we freeze into a permanent pattern of national superiority and inferiority that distinction between the "have" and the "have not" states which, however much it has been distorted and emphasized for partisan purposes, does nevertheless have a certain modicum of reason behind it. If, on the other hand, we add "industrial" resources, as the Dublin conference suggested, meaning supposedly such things as wealth and manufacturing capacity, we face very puzzling new questions. Again, exactly which resources shall we choose? And how shall we measure each of them?

Having measured each, we face an even more difficult question: how shall we correlate them in a common measuring stick? In some way we have to "weight" their relative importance. Alas, when we reach this particular stage in our appraisal of resources, we are pretty surely going to find that we are tending to rate high those resources, both natural and man-made, that are resources for making war, when we profess to be planning for a world at peace! Furthermore, we are going to find that many "natural resources", and particularly those that are *not* for making war—such resources, for example, as fertile soils, pleasant climate,

navigable rivers, and beautiful scenery—are impossibly
hard to evaluate at all, to say nothing of weighting
them relatively to other resources. And we are further
going to find also that some nations, such as Holland
for example, seem to have made a place for themselves
in the world out of all proportion to either their populations or their natural resources, while other nations,
possessed of large populations and of great wealths of
natural resources, have remained culturally and politically stagnant. In other words, there is grave question whether "resources" is, after all, a really valid
measuring stick.

It is this last objection, quite aside from the difficulties of valuation, of correlation, and of the undesirable
perpetuation of the *status quo,* that would seem to make
"resources" both an inadequate and an undesirable
basis for the allocation of world-state voting power.
This can best be shown by trying to apply it specifically.
The main natural resource of Switzerland is undoubtedly its scenery, of Hawaii its climate. It is clearly almost
impossibly difficult to set a value on either resource in
definite terms of any sort, and it is clearly still more
difficult to correlate either, in one concrete rating, with,
for example, the mineral wealth of Peru or New Caledonia. But, if we should, after all, attempt to make such
an evaluation and correlation, we would find that we
were running into a third difficulty. We would see that,
besides its mineral wealth, Peru has mountain scenery
which is probably quite as fine as that of Switzerland,
and that New Caledonia has a climate perhaps com-
parable to that of Hawaii. Yet, in the rating scale we
are making up, neither lesser known country is getting

any credit from us whatever for either "resource". Why? Because neither resource has been exploited and used, i.e. because neither has had added to it certain quite intangible human factors. In other words, what we discover is that it is these "intangible human factors" that are, in the last analysis, the really important thing. In our weighting of "resources" we are giving no consideration whatever to them; yet, without them, all "national resources" would be valueless. *They* are the vital inwardness of the importance that every nation has in, and to, the world. It is they, and not the resources at all, that we ought to try to put our fingers upon and to evaluate. But how?

III. THE NEW SOLUTION

S O MUCH for previous attempts to solve the Dilemma. Does this paucity of real solutions, this failure to meet the basic issue, mean that there exists no genuinely sound basis on which we can allocate voting power in a world-state? Let us see.

In the first place, what do we mean by a "sound" basis? We mean, it would seem, one:

1. That will appeal to the general opinion of the world as fundamentally equitable. To be that it must be a basis that will give to the great powers, and to the highly civilized smaller powers, a greater *proportion* of total world voting strength than their respective populations would entitle them to merely as populations:

2. That will, at the same time, be mutually protective, i.e. that will, on the one hand, protect the weaker states against the political domination, or the economic encroachment, of the greater ones; and that will, on the other hand, protect the more civilized states against what might be the more or less irresponsible voting of the mass populations of the (at present) backward states; and

3. That will (and this is perhaps most important of all) be *automatically adaptive to continually changing conditions,* i.e. one that will be able flexibly to correct its own initial errors, as, in practice, they may reveal themselves, and that will be able to make immediate

and logical adjustment to entirely new situations as, in practice, they may develop.

It is difficult to deny that our world-state ought to be the ultimate in democracy; and, in any democracy, as we have said, we cannot—that is we cannot if we have the faith of our convictions—ask, or care, whether a world-state voter be white, black, yellow or brown, whether he be Jew, Christian, Mohammedan or pagan, or whether he be democrat, royalist, socialist, communist or anarchist. But it is equally difficult to deny that we do have the right to ask, if he is going to vote upon something directly concerning ourselves, that he have some intellectual comprehension of the matter upon which he is voting! Perhaps a very slight comprehension, or a distorted comprehension, or a biased comprehension, but at least *some* comprehension. And, when we have rephrased the Great Dilemma in these terms, haven't we at the same time phrased the logical solution—in fact the unanswerable—solution, to it? Which is: that the voting power of each of the respective countries of the world in a world-state ought to be based, *not* upon population, or area, or natural resources, or wealth, or manufacturing capacity, or military strength, or upon anything whatsoever except a quality which no one has mentioned, viz. *the collective ability of its citizens to carry the responsibility of exercising for the common good its national franchise in the World-State*. And does not this mean, if we try to rephrase it in some way that will give it more concrete form, that national voting power should rest upon *the relative sum total of the educational accomplishment of all of the citizens of each country?*

This solution for the Dilemma has two very important arguments in its favor other than its logic: it is perhaps the only solution that can give no race, or country, or creed, or political ideology, any legitimate reason for offense. And it seems to be the only basis for world organization yet proposed that completely eliminates any element of *status quo,* but, instead, possesses what was termed above the automatically "self-corrective" element. For, once we adopt an educational basis for national voting powers in the World-State, we give hope to every backward people, race, and nation. No matter how low politically may be their present estate, the remedy for that low estate will lie, thereafter, to a very large degree indeed, in their own hands. If they want to increase their world power they will no longer have to raise armies and build battleships: they will have, instead, to decrease their own illiteracy and to increase the number, and to strengthen the work of their schools and colleges. This latter task, it is true, also takes brains and energy and money, but it takes far less of each than is required to build a nation up to great military power. In a single generation Russia has shown the tremendous strides that a country can make educationally if it really sets its heart to the task; and the road that Russia followed lies open to every presently backward state.

Obviously there are innumerable criticisms of detail that can be brought against this proposal. But, before we attempt to anticipate and to answer any of them, let us clear the ground by taking up very briefly three fundamental objections that will almost surely be raised against it.

The first of these is basically a moral one. It will be directed against educational selectiveness *per se*. We will be told that, since all men—white or black, educated or ignorant, clean or diseased, tolerant or fanatic—are "God's children", and therefore "equal" in His sight, they should all be given an equal vote in our World-State, regardless of their intelligence, or their lack of it, and even though this means an equal right to control, for good or ill, not only their destinies, but also our own. The fallacy inherent in this contention has, of course, been exposed a thousand times; but it is probably necessary, with the utmost brevity, to expose it again before we go further, for no recorded political dictum has been more misunderstood—either deliberately or unwittingly—than that continually quoted one that says that "all men are created equal." It ought to be unnecessary to point out that the authors of this famous phrase knew just as well as we do that all men are not "created equal" in such qualities as physical strength, and mental ability, and social background, and that the "equality" to which they referred in their dictum was solely one of equality before the law, of equality in the right, as they put it, to "life, liberty and the pursuit of happiness." No democracy thinks of assuming that all of its citizens are equally well equipped, morally and intellectually, to assume the responsibility of governing the lives of their fellow men. It does not even assume that they are equally well equipped to take that minor, but essential, share in governance that we call "voting": every democracy, without exception, disfranchises its young, its insane, and its criminals. In other words, the "right" to vote is not a natural, "God-given" right at all; it is a privilege, conferred by the whole body of the citizens of every democracy upon those of its own number whom it con-considers best able to exercise that privilege for the common good.

The second of the three fundamental objections that will be brought against using educational accomplishment as the basis of voting power in a new world order will undoubtedly be that it is unsound in its basic assumption. It will be asserted that education is not, of itself, any guarantee whatever of either personal morality or civic righteousness. And these objectors will point out, to prove that the exact contrary is true, that Germany, the most ruthless disturber of the world's peace in all history, has the highest "educational age" of any one of the great powers; and that Japan, Germany's partner, rose in three generations from being educationally one of the most backward of nations to being one of the most advanced. Nevertheless, obviously, despite these two disconcerting exhibits raised up against us, it is impossible for our critics seriously to contend: "*this* is what education does to a nation, therefore God forbid that we have any more of it!" It is clear enough, if we carry through to this *reductio ad absurdum*, that the trouble with Germany and Japan was not too much education but too little morals, i.e. too much education placed in the wrong hands and put to the wrong uses. We have to grant that education, of itself, is no guarantee of either good or evil; that what it does is to magnify all human powers to do either. Nevertheless, it still remains true that, however perverted may be the ends that education is sometimes asked to serve, the general trend of its influence—and this statement is based upon all recorded human experience—is *toward* tolerance, *toward* peace, *toward* health, *toward* happiness, in both the individual and the community.

IV. HOW IT CAN BE MADE POSSIBLE

T HE THIRD basic objection to any educational basis for world-state voting power is almost surely going to be that it is "impractical", i.e. that, although it may, in theory, have some validity, it would be both impossible to "sell" it, as a basis for world-state organization, to the various peoples of the world; and equally impossible to put it into working practice, even if we were able to convince these peoples of its desirability.

Argument on the first part of this objection has little value because there exists no data to base argument on. We have very little idea as to what the general popular reception of such a suggestion as this would be. A great deal would depend upon the auspices under which it was presented, the way in which it was presented, and the world-known individuals who approved, or objected, to it.

But our real question is not: "Will this proposal meet with general approval, or disapproval?" but rather: "Will it meet with more approval, or less approval, than any one of the alternative proposals that have been so far advanced?" We cannot escape the inevitable fact that, if we are to have a world-state at all, we must find *some* basis for allocating voting power in it. Our problem, therefore, is not an absolute but a relative one. We are not obliged to find a perfect solution, but to choose between alternative proposals, every one of which is admittedly imperfect.

Three alternative bases for allocating national voting power in a world-state have been so far suggested. We have seen that the first one—viz. national equality in voting power, with Guatemala, for example, having an equal power with, say Russia—has already been discarded by both the two leagues of nations as admittedly farcical. We have seen that the second basis—viz. voting power based on population, with India, for example, outvoting Europe—would also probably never be accepted by any one. And we have discussed the third basis—viz. voting power based on "resources". But it is clear that we could raise against each of these three proposals the same additional objections that have just been raised against our educational proposal. Would, for instance, the great masses of the peoples of the world understand a voting-power formula based on "resources"—even if the experts proved able to work one out—any better than they might understand one based on "education"? And would "resources", as a basis, have any more popular appeal to the plain people of the world than "education"?

The second half of the objection of "impracticability" is another sort of a matter. And, instead of discussing it in vague generalities, let us bring it down to earth by outlining some of the specific methods and procedures that *might* be used in making our proposal concrete. Then we at least shall have something definite to discuss. Before we can do this, however, we shall have to settle several preliminary questions, some of them very important ones.

One of the first of these preliminary questions is: how far should we go—that is into how much detail should we go—in weighing a nation's "educational accomplishment"? Should we simply—as, indeed, several plans have already proposed—count its literate population, i.e., those able to read and write, in any language? It would seem that the answer to this question ought to be "No". And to show why it ought to be "No," an actual example may be cited. The United States with 139,000,000 inhabitants, has at present some eighty million adult literates. China, with 480,000,000 inhabitants, is also represented to have at present eighty million or more adult literates. In other words, on a literacy basis alone, China would have a voting power equal to that of the United States. But the United States is, as a country, educationally matured: even if it went "all out" in a sustained drive to eliminate illiteracy, it probably would not be able to add over three per cent to its literacy total. On the other hand, by making the same sort of a drive over a similar period, China might easily double its literate population. Would this mean that *then* it would be wise to give China, in the world-state, a voting power double that of the United States? And by "wise" I mean: would the world as a whole, or even China itself, be better off if it were given such a voting power? We can admit that, by the doubling of its literate population, China would greatly increase its world stature—socially, culturally, and economically— and that it should be granted, for that accomplishment, a much greater world voting power. But does that mean that, with a doubled literacy, it should have a *doubled* voting power? Suppose it became 100% literate, but progressed no further along the educational road than *that*: it would obviously still be a long way indeed from

being as important to the well-being of the world as
the United States is at present.

We must never forget that what we are trying to develop is some sort of reasonably valid "measuring stick"
of the very real, but very vaguely defined, concept that
we call "national importance". Suppose, to make this
particular point clearer, that we consider for a moment
the other end of our educational scale, that we look at
the top of it instead of the bottom, i.e. at the holders
of doctoral degrees in any country. (And, for our purposes here, let us try entirely to forget about them as
either individuals, or as individual voters: let us think
of them as an instrument, as simply a device to measure
with.) Are the holders of doctoral degrees of a given
country a "reasonably valid" index to its world importance or are they not? We know that, numerically,
they are a very insignificant fraction indeed of the total
population of every country. Nevertheless it will probably be found to be the fact that there is no single statistical index to the relative world importance of a nation—in all its aspects—which is more accurate than
the number of its holders of doctoral degrees. And
the reason for this is that, culturally speaking, its doctors are literally the "leaven that leaveneth the whole
lump"; and that, as such, they are an almost uncannily
correct reflection of the relative place of each nation
in the world. Tell me the number of doctors of medi-
cine that any country has, per thousand of its population, and I will be able to tell you at once about how
that country stands, relatively to all others, in medical
care and hospital facilities, in medical research and
disease prevention, in personal hygiene and infant

mortality, in sanitation and public health. Tell me the number of its doctors of science and philosophy and of graduate engineers, per thousand of its population, and I can rate for you its relative industrial productivity and its wealth, its relative military strength and its standard of living. Tell me the number of its doctors of education and law and theology and music and the arts, and I can tell you at once whether it is, as a nation, one of the cultural leaders of the world or one of the followers.

But, if sheer literacy is of fundamental importance— as it is; and, if the educational "top" of the scale also has high statistical validity—as it has; we logically arrive at the conclusion that, if we are to weigh a country educationally at all, we ought to weigh it at all of our educational levels, i.e. we ought to give it credit for everything, educationally speaking, that it has accomplished. No other statistical method is going to give a fair picture of its relative cultural standing as a nation.

But, it will be immediately asked, in what possible way can we get at and measure the "total educational accomplishment" of a given country? Theoretically this isn't so hard. Actually there are a number of possible statistical methods that we might use, some more exact, some less so. For our purposes here, however, we may take one obvious and logical one: we may measure total national accomplishment in terms of *the total of the years of the individual educational accomplishment of each one of its citizens*. Which means—to rephrase our method in the simplest terms—that we might allow each nation one year of "accomplishment

credit" for each member of its barely literate population; four years of "credit" for each member of its population who had completed the equivalent of the first
half of an American elementary school education;
eight years credit for each member who had completed
a full elementary, or "grammar school", education;
twelve years for each one with a high school education; sixteen years for each one who was a college
graduate; and nineteen years for each one who had
acquired any one of the various doctoral degrees.

Our "practical" critics will come back at us at this
point with all sorts of objections to this particular method. They will say that it is "doctrinnaire"—whatever
that means!; that it provides for too many educational
levels (or for too few!) that the difference in the credit
allowed the various classes is too great (or too little);
that informal education ought not to be counted for
credit (or that it ought to be); that differentiation
should be made between various types, or even subject
matters, of education (or that there shouldn't be any
such a differentiation), etc., etc., etc.

This sort of criticism seems to me, at this particular
stage, beside the point. It is not being contended that
the particular method just summarized for computing
total national "educational accomplishment" is the best
possible one that can be developed. It is submitted here
simply as one possible method, as a logical and under-
standable method, and as a reasonably simple one.
Granted that it may be possible later to work out a better one; at least here is a method sufficiently under-
standable to form a reasonably valid basis for our
proposal.

Or our critics may admit that this method is one that may have some theoretical validity, but they will follow up this admission with another easy criticism. They will assert that, if we have any idea of applying it on a world-wide scale, we would be attempting something statistically too enormous and too complex ever to be reducible to workable practice. There is just one good way to answer this sort of criticism: and that is to show —even though it be in very rough and tentative form— the result that they tell us it is quite impossible for us to secure at all, i.e. to present a picture of the various countries of the world as they would appear when we have worked out, to the best of our present ability, their respective total "educational accomplishments".

The construction of this picture (Table C.) was, it must be admitted, a very considerable statistical task, even in the admittedly "rough and tentative form" in which we have described it. The procedure followed in making it was, however, simple enough. First, an analysis of the educational accomplishment of each separate country was made, to the degree that statistics were available for it. And, to show exactly how this first stage of the work was carried through in the case of a country which had available statistics, let us take as a sample the United States itself, (Table B.).

TABLE B.

Method Used in Computing The "Total Educational Accomplishment" of a Country, and its Average "Educational Age," in Cases Where Fairly Complete Statistics are Available.

This table takes the United States as a sample country, and these figures are for the adult literate population of the United States for the year 1945. Even these figures for the U. S. are only estimates made from the best data obtainable. The latest census statistics available are those for 1940, not 1945; are for adults of 25 years old and over, not 21 years. Also they record years of formal school work taken, not educational accomplishment however acquired, and require other adjustments taken from supplementary data. Since any errors in estimate tend to cancel each other out, the net results are, probably, reasonably near correct.

	Number of literate adults (21 years and over) who have completed the years of education stated.	Translation into net "years," of "educational accomplishment" (i.e. the population of the age group multiplied by the number of years of the group's accomplishment.)
1 year completed	500,000	500,000
2 years completed	1,000,000	2,000,000
3 years completed	2,000,000	6,000,000
4 years completed (i.e. completion of the first half of elementary school—but no further)	3,000,000	12,000,000
5 years completed	5,000,000	25,000,000
6 years completed	5,000,000	30,000,000
7 years completed	8,000,000	56,000,000
8 years completed (i.e. completion of grammar school, but no further)	21,000,000	168,000,000

	Number of literate adults (21 years and over) who have completed the years of education stated.	Translation into net "years" of "educational accomplishment" (i.e. the population of the age group multiplied by the number of years of the group's accomplishment.)
9 years completed	6,000,000	54,000,000
10 years completed	4,000,000	40,000,000
11 years completed	3,000,000	33,000,000
12 years completed (i.e. completion of high school, but no further)	12,000,000	144,000,000
13 years completed	3,000,000	39,000,000
14 years completed	1,500,000	21,000,000
15 years completed	500,000	7,500,000
16 years completed (i.e. completion of college, but no further)	2,500,000	40,000,000
17 years completed	600,000	10,200,000
18 years completed	300,000	5,400,000
19 years or more completed (i.e. posssession of a doctoral degree)	400,000	7,600,000
Total adult literate population	79,300,000	
Total "educational years" of the country's adult literate population		701,200,000
Average education (in years) of the country's adult literates. This we here term the country's average "educational age."		8.9

Having compiled a whole series of similar tables (using, so far as the statistical data available permitted, the form used in "Table B.") for each one of the seventy-four countries listed in "Table A.", and, having tabulated the net results of each of these seventy-four preliminary tables into one table, we arrive at "Table C.", which presents the "picture" we set out to develop.

TABLE C.

THE COUNTRIES OF THE WORLD WITH THEIR POPULATIONS "WEIGHTED" ACCORDING TO THEIR "EDUCATIONAL AGE."

In other words showing their respective total "educational accomplishments." The "educational age" of each country has been derived for it separately in accordance with the method used in "Table B" so far as data was available to use this method; in other cases by the interpolation and extrapolation of fragmentary data; in a few cases by sheer estimate. "Min." in this table means "not known even approximately, but almost certainly not having a sufficient educational accomplishment to qualify the country in question for more than one World Assembly Representative."

	Column A. Estimated Population (from Table A.)	Column B. Estimated Adult literate population	Column C. "Educational Age" of Country (i.e. Average literate adult educational accomplishment, in years.)	Column D. Total number of "Educational years" of National Accomplishment (i.e. Column B. multiplied by Column C.)
United States	140,000,000	79,300,000	8.9	705,770,000
Russia	188,000,000	93,200,000	5.0	466,000,000
Great Britain	47,000,000	26,200,000	8.4	220,080,000
Ireland	3,000,000	1,600,000	7.2	11,520,000
British India	396,000,000	14,000,000	3.3	46,200,000
Australia	7,300,000	3,800,000	8.6	32,680,000
New Zealand	1,700,000	900,000	8.6	7,740,000
South Africa	10,000,000	3,500,000	3.6	12,600,000
Canada	12,000,000	6,500,000	7.6	49,400,000

Rest of British Colonies ..	89,000,000	5,000,000	3.1	15,500,000
Total for British Empire ..	566,000,000	61,500,000		395,720,000
China	480,000,000	70,000,000	2.2	154,000,000
Holland (incl. colonies) ..	77,000,000	9,000,000	6.5	58,500,000
Italy	46,000,000	20,000,000	5.1	102,000,000
France (incl. colonies) ...	135,000,000	26,400,000	6.9	182,160,000
Portugal (incl. colonies) ..	15,000,000	Min.		Min.
Germany	70,000,000	38,000,000	9.1	345,800,000
Belgium (incl. colonies) ..	18,000,000	4,200,000	8.9	37,380,000
Spain (incl. colonies)	29,000,000	10,000,000	4.8	48,000,000
Luxembourg	Min.	Min.		Min.
Switzerland	4,300,000	2,400,000	9.0	21,600,000
Denmark	3,900,000	2,200,000	9.2	20,240,000
Norway	2,900,000	1,700,000	9.0	15,300,000
Sweden	6,600,000	3,900,000	9.1	35,490,000
Finland	3,800,000	2,100,000	8.2	17,220,000
Latvia	1,600,000	Min.		Min.
Estonia	1,000,000	Min.		Min.
Lithuania	2,700,000	Min.		Min.
Poland	28,000,000	14,000,000	5.0	70,000,000
Czechoslovakia	10,000,000	6,000,000	7.2	43,200,000
Austria	5,800,000	3,200,000	8.6	27,520,000
Hungary	13,000,000	6,800,000	6.9	46,920,000
Rumania	9,000,000	Min.		Min.

	Column A. Estimated Population (from Table A.)	Column B. Estimated Adult literate population	Column C. "Educational Age" of Country (i.e. Average literate adult educational accomplishment, in years.)	Column D. Total number of "Educational years" of National Accomplishment (i.e. Column B. multiplied by Column C.)
Bulgaria	6,600,000	Min.		Min.
Albania	Min.	Min.		Min.
Greece	6,000,000	Min.		Min.
Jugoslavia	15,000,000	5,000,000	2.5	12,500,000
Japan	72,000,000	39,000,000	3.8	148,200,000
Korea	23,000,000	Min.		Min.
Philippines	16,000,000	Min.		Min.
Siam	15,000,000	Min.		Min.
Afghanistan	12,000,000	Min.		Min.
Persia	14,000,000	Min.		Min.
Iraq	5,000,000	Min.		Min.
Arabia	5,000,000	Min.		Min.
Turkey	17,000,000	Min.		Min.
Syria & Lebanon	4,000,000	Min.		Min.
Egypt	16,000,000	Min.		Min.
Ethiopia	12,000,000	Min.		Min.
Liberia	1,500,000	Min.		Min.
Brazil	42,000,000	14,000,000	4.3	60,200,000
Argentina	14,000,000	6,000,000	4.5	27,000,000

Chile	5,000,000	Min.		Min.
Uruguay	2,000,000	Min.		Min.
Paraguay	1,000,000	Min.		Min.
Bolivia	3,000,000	Min.		Min.
Ecuador	3,000,000	Min.		Min.
Peru	6,000,000	Min.		Min.
Colombia	9,000,000	Min.		Min.
Venezuela	4,000,000	Min.		Min.
Panama	600,000	Min.		Min.
Costa Rica	600,000	Min.		Min.
Guatemala	3,500,000	Min.		Min.
Honduras	1,000,000	Min.		Min.
Salvador	2,200,000	Min.		Min.
Nicaragua	1,000,000	Min.		Min.
Cuba	4,400,000	Min.		Min.
Haiti	3,000,000	Min.		Min.
Dominican Republic	1,700,000	Min.		Min.
Mexico	20,000,000	7,000,000	4.1	28,700,000
Other parts of the world ..	12,000,000	Min.		Min.
Est. totals for all "Min." countries		30,000,000		60,000,000
TOTALS	2,235,700,000	554,900,000		3,129,420,000

V. THE QUESTION OF EXACT STATISTICAL ACCURACY

B EFORE we go any further it will probably be wise to discuss in somewhat more detail the objection that we can do nothing whatever to set up any sort of an educational basis for voting power unless and until we have exact and world-wide statistics for it.

The first answer to this objection is that it goes too far, for, if it be valid, no world-state is possible on *any* basis (except one giving an equal vote to each nation); for the same statistical objections that can be raised against "education" can be raised against every other allocated-voting-power basis that has been proposed. For every one of them we lack, equally or even more, exact and complete statistical data. Yet it is difficult to believe that we are obliged to give up all hope of establishing a world-state simply for lack of enough statistics. There must be ways of getting around this sort of a difficulty—temporarily at least. I believe that there are such ways; and particularly I believe that there are such ways in the case of educational statistics.

It must be frankly admitted at the start that the statistics quoted in "Table C." are of very unequal authenticity indeed, even though into the compiling of them there went a great deal of tedious delving into hundreds of volumes of source materials of a score of different types. No amount of bibliological research is going to secure for us what doesn't exist. Even the figures for the United States cited in Tables "B." and "C." are estimated ones only; and it is impossible from any data now available to make them anything more than estimated ones. If this is true of the United States, which provides us with a lavish wealth of educational statistical material, how much more is it true of other countries, for many of which statistics even of population are non-existent. For many countries that have some educational statistics they are extremely fragmentary. For very few countries indeed are they complete enough to enable one to make, with anything like an approach to accuracy, the graded breakdown that "Table C." calls for.

But we are not to blame for the world's lack of statistics. We would be to blame, however, if we allowed that lack to cause us to make no attempt to solve the puzzling problem that we are absolutely obliged —somehow—to solve. To sit down and do nothing— considering the driving need that we face—would seem to me nothing more nor less than a form of intellectual cowardice. Suppose we don't have exact figures for a given country; we can—and it seems to me that we should—develop the best estimated ones that we can, basing our estimates on whatever information we can get.

Take such a country as Ethiopia. There appear to be no published educational statistics whatever for it. But that does not mean that we know absolutely nothing about the educational status of Ethiopia. We have such things as consular reports from Ethiopia and the letters of missionaries; we have the records of

travellers and the reports of war correspondents and
newspaper men. And from all of these materials we
can piece together an impression, and a fairly definite
impression at that, of the educational situation in that
particular country. And from that impression we can
venture, and venture with fair assurance, at least
this opinion: that Ethiopia ranks so low in national
"educational accomplishment" that it comes within
what "Table C." terms the "minimum" class.

That we may rely on estimation at least to this extent our statistical critics will probably agree. They
will probably admit that indirect evidence of the
sort just cited may, after all, be sufficient to enable
us to place a given country in the "minimum" class.
But even this admission accomplishes a good deal, for
it actually takes care for us of about half of all of
the countries in the world. At this point, however,
our statistical critics are likely to stop their conces-
sions: from there they will probably continue to assert
that for us to use estimative methods of this sort in
the establishment of the "educational accomplishment"
of any one of the great powers is not going to obtain
very satisfactory results.

Of course it isn't. No one claims that it will. All
that one claims is that a careful estimate for any
country, based on all the best data obtainable for it,
is better than no estimate at all. Take this question
of educational estimation at its present worst: consider
the chief unknown quantities among the great powers,
China and Russia. Probably some one in the Soviet
Union knows something approximately correct about
that country's present educational accomplishment.

We do have some statistics; but they are incomplete, mutually contradictory, and—like so much other data of Russian origin—subject to semantic interpretation. For China we have practically no published educational statistics whatever: for it we are obliged, to the best of our ability, practically to guess. Admittedly then, for each of these two countries, the figures in "Table C." may be very much wrong: they may be very much too high or very much too low. On the other hand, they may be exactly right!

We must never forget, also, that there is such a thing as rating statistical exactitude too highly. Figures do lie. And absolute exactitude is a chimera, something forever impossible, of attainment. Suppose that every separate country were able to supply us with absolutely complete and absolutely exact statistics. Not even then could we compile an exactly correct "Table C." Why not? Because we would still have to correlate the highly individualized statistics of seventy-odd countries into a single integrated table. And this could not be done *exactly* because it would involve the reduction of seventy inherently incommensurable sets of figures to a series of common denominators. We would have to determine what, in the educational system of India for example, constitutes "literacy"; to determine what, in the educational system of Germany for example, is the "equivalent" of an American "college" education, etc. No series of correlations such as these could possibly be other than a series of careful approximations.

For "exactness" and "accuracy" are always relative terms. We approximate each only to such a degree as the demand of the work in hand justifies. It conceivably would be possible (and, at some time in the future, it conceivably might be desirable) to attempt a world-wide registration of voters according to a uniform and carefully organized plan. The difficulties in consummating such a registration would be great but not insuperable, the cost enormous but bearable, the results unquestionably more accurate than those which we are able to arrive at today from the fragmentary data that we have. Following such a census, some countries would probably lose representatives in a World-Assembly which had been partly based on estimate, and some would gain them. It is therefore clearly important that, even at the start, "Table C." be made as nearly accurate as it is possible, with the means and the time at our disposal, to make it. But, at the same time, we must keep in mind this mental reservation: that no inaccuracies in statistical detail, however serious, can impair the validity of our basic plan—as a plan. No matter what plan we adopted we would want to eliminate errors of estimation, as fast as we could—of course; but that does not mean that we should discard any plan as unworkable just because it is unable, at the beginning, for reasons quite beyond our control, completely to rid itself of them.

Suppose we had sought to develop a "Table C." based on "wealth", wealth, as a "measuring stick" for national voting power, having been, as we remember, proposed by a number of world-state advocates. Would this change of basis solve all our statistical difficulties? Quite the contrary. It would introduce us to a lot of new ones that "education," as a basis, knows nothing about. Before it is possible for us to attempt to measure anything we have to agree upon a definition of the thing we are trying to measure. And here, as compared with "education," "wealth" starts off seriously handicapped, because there is a profound lack of agreement among the experts as to what the wealth of a country consists of. It consists of so many different sorts of things, of lands and buildings, and of their contents, of railroads and public utilities and ships and automobiles, of raw materials in storage, in transit, and in process. But are bank deposits, and stocks and bonds, and currency, "wealth?" We have to be careful, or we'll find ourselves counting wealth twice. And what of our unmined coal, our unpumped oil, our future water-power potential: surely all these things are a part of national wealth. But how, at the present time, are we going to evaluate them *exactly?* And what of those other national "assets" we mentioned a chapter or two back, such things as scenery and climate?

If we should try to take "wealth" as a basis all these questions would be preliminary, questions of definition. If and when we had finally reached an agreement on them we would still face every one of the purely statistical difficulties that face us now in our attempted evaluation of "educational accomplishment." As a matter of fact, no matter what measuring stick we decided to use—whether it were population, or resources, or wealth, or educational accomplishment, or something else—we would, with each, face the same difficulties of definition, the same difficulties of evaluation, and the same paucity of exact and complete data.

But, finally, and this is by far the most important fact of all the facts about it, "Table C." is, with an "educational" basis, automatically subject to continual revision, correction and adjustment to changing situations. Of no other basis is this so true. This essentiality of it will be further discussed in a later chapter.

VI. THE TRANSLATION OF OUR "YARDSTICK" INTO POLITICAL PRACTICE

Table "C." is obviously only a preliminary step. Even if we accept it as at least correct enough to serve as a basis for argument, it is necessary for us to translate its statistics into political practice. Fortunately, this step is a simple one. If we assume—again to be concrete in our proposals—that our proposed World-State is to be governed by a one-chamber Assembly, then, in this Assembly, under the plan here being proposed, each nation would have as many representatives as, relative to all other nations, its "educational accomplishment" entitled it to. How would we arrive at the number of its representatives?

Very easily indeed. We would divide the total number of seats that we propose our "World Assembly" to have, whatever we may decide that number to be, into the total "educational accomplishment" of the entire world. For, under our plan, the "constituency" of each World Assembly representative will be, not a constituency of so many millions of voters, but a constituency of (voters possessing) so many millions of total years of educational accomplishment. This phraseology makes the thing sound a bit complicated when it really isn't. What happens—and it happens automatically—is exactly the result, the crucially important result, that we want to bring about: namely that all the highly educated countries get a large representation in the World Assembly, because each of their representatives represents relatively few voters; while the highly illiterate countries get slender representation in the Assembly, because each of their representatives represents relatively many voters.

But *how many* representatives for each country? Well, using "Table C." as it stands, for one set of factors, and arbitrarily assuming for our purposes here, that our new World Assembly is to have an initial membership of four hundred members,* then each nation listed in "Table C." will have the representation in this World Assembly that is set forth in "Table D." below. In "Table D." the countries have been re-arranged in the order of the number of their World-State representatives, i. e. in the order of their respective voting power—at the start—in the new World-State. (Note, by the way, the phrase "at the start"; for this qualification is, as we shall see, extremely important.)

---

* Over four hundred members are shown in the total of "Table D.". This is due to a suggested supplementary rule, viz. that each presently independent country, no matter how small its educational strength, shall have at least one representative. To that extent concession is made to present "sovereignty"!

TABLE D.

NUMBER OF REPRESENTATIVES IN A "WORLD ASSEMBLY" ALLOTTED TO EACH OF THE COUNTRIES OF THE WORLD ON THE BASIS OF THEIR RESPECTIVE NATIONAL TOTALS OF "EDUCATIONAL ACCOMPLISHMENT"

Arranged here in the order of their standing in educational accomplishment, and so in the order of their voting power. Every "sovereign" country listed to have at least one representative, even if only fractionally entitled to one.

	Estimated Total Population (from Table A.)	Estimated Adult Literate Population (from Table C.)	Estimated Total Educational Accomplishment (In Adult literate years) (from Table C.)	No. of World assembly representatives
United States	140,000,000	79,300,000	705,770,000	88
Russia	188,000,000	93,200,000	466,000,000	59
British Empire	566,000,000	61,500,000	395,720,000	49
Germany	70,000,000	38,000,000	345,800,000	44
French Empire	135,000,000	26,400,000	182,160,000	22
China	480,000,000	70,000,000	154,000,000	20
Japan	72,000,000	39,000,000	148,200,000	18
Italy	46,000,000	20,000,000	102,000,000	13
Poland	28,000,000	14,000,000	70,000,000	9
Brazil ....?	42,000,000	14,000,000	60,200,000	8
Holland (incl. colonies) .	77,000,000	9,000,000	58,500,000	7
Spain (incl. colonies) ...	29,000,000	10,000,000	48,000,000	6
Hungary	13,000,000	6,800,000	46,920,000	6
Czechoslovakia	10,000,000	6,000,000	43,200,000	5

	Estimated Total Population (from Table A.)	Estimated Adult Literate Population (from Table C.)	Estimated Total Educational Accomplishment (In Adult literate years) (from Table C.)	No. of World assembly representatives
Belgium (incl. colonies) .	18,000,000	4,200,000	37,380,000	4
Sweden	6,600,000	3,900,000	35,490,000	4
Mexico	20,000,000	7,000,000	28,700,000	4
Austria	5,800,000	3,200,000	27,520,000	4
Argentina	14,000,000	6,000,000	27,000,000	4
Switzerland	4,300,000	2,400,000	21,600,000	3
Denmark	3,900,000	2,200,000	20,240,000	3
Finland	3,800,000	2,100,000	17,220,000	2
Norway	2,900,000	1,700,000	15,300,000	2
Jugoslavia	15,000,000	5,000,000	12,500,000	2
Rumania	9,000,000	Min.	Min.	1
Chile	5,000,000	Min.	Min.	1
Philippines	16,000,000	Min.	Min.	1
Lithuania	2,700,000	Min.	Min.	1
Cuba	4,400,000	Min.	Min.	1
Bulgaria	6,600,000	Min.	Min.	1
Turkey	17,000,000	Min.	Min.	1
Colombia	9,000,000	Min.	Min.	1
Portugal (incl. colonies) .	15,000,000	Min.	Min.	1
Greece	6,000,000	Min.	Min.	1
Latvia	1,600,000	Min.	Min.	1
Uruguay	2,000,000	Min.	Min.	1
Peru	6,000,000	Min.	Min.	1
Estonia	1,000,000	Min.	Min.	1

Siam	15,000,000	Min.	Min.	Min.	1
Venezuela	4,000,000	Min.	Min.	Min.	1
Luxembourg	300,000	Min.	Min.	Min.	1
Korea	23,000,000	Min.	Min.	Min.	1
Egypt	16,000,000	Min.	Min.	Min.	1
Persia	14,000,000	Min.	Min.	Min.	1
Guatemala	3,500,000	Min.	Min.	Min.	1
Ecuador	3,000,000	Min.	Min.	Min.	1
Bolivia	3,000,000	Min.	Min.	Min.	1
Honduras	1,000,000	Min.	Min.	Min.	1
Salvador	2,200,000	Min.	Min.	Min.	1
Costa Rica	600,000	Min.	Min.	Min.	1
Panama	600,000	Min.	Min.	Min.	1
Paraguay	1,000,000	Min.	Min.	Min.	1
Syria & Lebanon	4,000,000	Min.	Min.	Min.	1
Dominican Republic	1,700,000	Min.	Min.	Min.	1
Nicaragua	1,000,000	Min.	Min.	Min.	1
Albania	1,000,000	Min.	Min.	Min.	1
Iraq	5,000,000	Min.	Min.	Min.	1
Arabia	5,000,000	Min.	Min.	Min.	1
Liberia	1,500,000	Min.	Min.	Min.	1
Haiti	3,000,000	Min.	Min.	Min.	1
Afghanistan	12,000,000	Min.	Min.	Min.	1
Ethiopia	12,000,000	Min.	Min.	Min.	1
Other parts of world	12,000,000	Min.	Min.	Min.	—
TOTALS	2,237,000,000		524,900,000	3,069,420,000	424

This last table completes the rough outline of our proposed solution for the Dilemma, our endeavor to find what we termed a "sound" method of establishing respective national powers in our new World-State. Study "Table D." Note the relative voting strengths which, under this plan, each nation might have. Some of them may seem out of position; but, on the whole, the table would appear to reflect rather closely the actual world strength and world importance of the various nations. We said above "rough outline": there still remain a number of questions to answer.

A very important first one of these questions is: will the various nations elect, each as a whole, its group of one or more representatives to the World Assembly? My own feeling is that the answer to this question ought, and ought very emphatically, to be "No." As I see it, each nation should, instead, be split up, by the Committee on Elections of the World-State into as many separate "World Electoral Districts" as its national quota of representatives entitles it to, and then that each of these World Electoral Districts should, independently, elect *its* representative to the World Assembly. You will notice, by the way, that each of these Electoral Districts would, under the plan, be delimited in such a way as to include within its boundaries, *not an approximately equal number of voters, but such a number of voters as will give to every Electoral District a number of voters having substantially an equal number of years of total "educational accomplishment."* And this in turn would mean—and this also would happen entirely automatically—that the voters of the more highly educated Electoral Districts would, on the average, have much more individual voting power in the new World-State than the voters in the barely literate Electoral Districts would have—which, of course, is one of the indirect but desirable results that we want to bring about.

Given our basic plan, a second question is sure, sooner or later, to be raised: do we propose to "weight" each voter's *individual* vote according to his or her individual educational accomplishment. Now, of course, this idea of basing individual voting power on educational ability is a very old and very intriguing one; but, for several reasons, the answer to it here almost surely ought also to be "No."

For one thing, there would be the very practical difficulties already alluded to, which, for the present at least, stand in the way of any world-wide registration of voters, to say nothing of a recording of their individual educational accomplishments. Our world voting system could easily become hopelessly bogged down in initial procedural detail.

But that isn't the main reason why a weighting of individual voting power is undesirable. The main reason is that it befogs what we are here trying to do. We are not setting up an educational measuring stick in order to give increased World-State voting power to educationally advanced individual voters. We are not even setting it up to give increased voting power to educationally advanced countries. To phrase the plan that way is to substitute *purpose* for *method*. What we are seeking to do is to work out some form of measuring stick which will, most equitably and most wisely, allocate voting power between the various nations: their relative educational accomplishments seem to be such a criterion. If we use that criterion we do give educationally advanced nations increased voting power; but that result is a result, not a purpose.

Against the giving of increased individual voting power to educationally advanced individuals—whatever the theoretical reasons favoring it—there are strong psychological and social arguments. It is difficult to deny that a highly educated country is more important in and to the world than an almost illiterate country. But this is far different from assuming that every grammar school graduate is, in his political thinking, twice as intelligent as an elementary school graduate, or that, even on the average, the social and political perspicacity of a college graduate is twice as great as that of a grammar school graduate. Theoretically it *ought* to be greater—in some proportion. Probably, on the average, it *is* greater. But I am very much afraid that to weight it, individually, on the assumption that it is, would be considered by those derated a sort of educational arrogance. For there is another factor that comes into the picture, a very old-fashioned, and at the present time often forgotten, factor, known as common sense. And common sense doesn't result from "schooling."

For every reason then it would seem to be wise to have all voters, the world over, simply cast *a* vote. The result would be that in each Electoral District all votes would have an equal voting power, and that that power would be determined by the total educational accomplishment of the District in which the votes are cast. We would thus avoid any question of what might be termed personal educational snobbishness on the one hand, and personal jealousy of educational prerogative on the other. In every high-educational-age District the barely literate voter would share in the high-power vote in the World-State which his highly educated neighbors have been able to secure for him. And this would please him, both personally and patriotically On the other hand, in every low-educational-age District, the highly educated voter would share in the low-power vote in the World-State which his barely literate neighbors have imposed upon *him*. And this would dissatisfy him. But, also, it ought to make him—a man who should be a leader in his District—inspired, and inspired both individually and patriotically, to work all the harder to raise the educational status of his neighbors.

VII. BRINGING THE NEW WORLD-STATE INTO BEING

Finally we come to our third, and last question of detail: what is our initial procedure going to be? How may we go about bringing into being such a new World-State as the one we are now talking about? In general it would seem to be altogether wise to try to work for it through the United Nations Organization, i.e. to use what we already have as a bridge toward getting something better. And, if you ask exactly how this might be done, here are a few suggestions as to the successive steps that *might* be taken:

1. Once the United Nations Organization has cleaned up what might be termed the most pressing problems left it by the war, and otherwise deemed itself ready to evolve into a true World-State, it might appoint two committees, one on World-State Constitution, one on World-State Elections.

2. The Committee on Constitution would be a widely representative committee made up from the Assembly's own membership. It would proceed to draft a new Constitution, and this time not a constitution for a league of *nations*, but a constitution for a World-State of *individuals*. This could be a relatively short, and relatively very simple, document, limiting itself closely to a few absolute fundamentals. This draft constitution would then be submitted to the Assembly

of the United Nations Organization; and, when—perhaps amended—it had been passed by it, it could, and of course would have to be, submitted to each member nation for its acceptance. Furthermore, acceptance of it by each country ought to be a voluntary matter; no World-State ought to begin operation under the shadow of coercion. On the other hand it could begin —after a fashion—when any two nations decided to go into it, and it could begin thus easily because it would be entirely possible for other nations to join with them in it at any time they chose. We may, however, strongly hope, and indeed we may believe, that the peoples of most of the smaller countries of the world at least are ready *now* to join such a World-State.

3. Meanwhile the other Committee, that on World Elections, would be at work. This committee would be composed, not of Assembly members, but of admitted experts in education, in statistics, and in political methodology. It also should be one of from ten to twenty-five members, i.e. large enough to be broadly representative of all classes, countries, and races.

4. This Elections Committee would forthwith invite each country which had accepted membership in the new World-State to submit to it detailed estimates of its own national educational accomplishment (i.e. a "Table B." for itself). In fact, it would ask each country to provide it with a whole series of "Table B.'s," not only one for itself as a whole, but a separate one for each one of its separate territories, counties, departments, states, provinces, or other divisions of itself, whatever they may be called. (This national

breakdown would be to aid the Committee in its delimitation of Electoral Districts.)   All of these tables would have, of course, to be just as fully authenticated and documented as possible. They would always be subject to impeachment by the Committee, to question and to verification.

5. For the *first* election to the Assembly of the new World-State this Committee on World Elections would be given full and unqualified power to decide, by its own majority vote, each country's quota of representatives.   And, having made this decision, it would, also by its own majority vote, have unqualified power to divide each country up into the one or more Electoral Districts to which its representation entitled it.   And for this *first* election there would be no appeal from the Committee's decisions.

Now it will be objected at once that this is altogether too vast and too arbitrary a power to put into the hands of this Committee, or of any Committee. Why, what we are really proposing here is that *it* settle the whole business of national representation! How do we know that it would exercise such a power as this wisely, or even honestly?   Here we are proposing that the entire Dilemma be solved by this Committee, and solved in so simple, so quick and so easy a manner that it might almost be described as off-hand.   But there are reasons why this procedure is entirely defendable.   We want to get our new World-State launched promptly.   We want to avoid at the start endless preliminary debate—and perhaps the creation of permanent hard feeling—over details of national representation and voting power.   But the

main reason why we can make all our initial determinations so casually—i.e by a plain majority vote of
one single committee—is a very simple one: under
our plan—and this, you will remember, is one of its
vital and outstanding advantages—all the determinations of the Elections Committee are purely temporary. In this new World-State of ours there are no
permanent *status quos*, no "freezing" of anything.
For the second election to the World Assembly all of
the Election Committee's representations, all of its
voting quotas, all of its Electoral District boundaries,
everything it does, will be reconsidered and determined all over again by an entirely new committee.
Furthermore, after the first election, it may—and probably would—be desirable to have all Election Committee decisions subject to appeal to, and review by,
the Assembly as a whole, and, perhaps, surrounded
by other precautionary safe-guards. This completely
temporary quality inherent in all Election Committee
decisions explains why, even if there is, at the start,
a certain amount of estimate, or even of arbitrariness,
in them, they can do no irreparable damage.

It is this fluidity that is the outstanding difference
between our new World-State and its predecessor
Leagues. Our new world organization will be a living,
growing organism. Its Committee on Elections will
be required at regular intervals to measure the world's
educational growth; and to reallocate each nation's
representation, and its voting power in the World-
State accordingly. Furthermore, with each such re-
appraisal, the world's educational statistics—with such
a spot light as this thrown on them!—are bound to

become more complete, more accurate, and more uniform, and the Committee itself more familiar with its duties and procedures. As a result its determinations are bound to become more accurate, and less subject to valid criticism. And, meanwhile, we have got the World-State launched!

6. Having set educational quotas, and having established World Electoral Districts, the Committee would permit each District, for the first world election, to nominate its own candidates for the World Assembly, and to conduct its own election for it, in any way it sees fit. Again this casualness does no irreparable damage. We get the World-State going. And, for later elections, the Elections Committee, or the Assembly itself, could—and probably would—desire to establish uniform world-wide election procedures.

7. On a given day the peoples of the world would meet to elect their representatives to the World Assembly. And, at some time later, these representatives would meet, and, by due process, the new World-State Assembly would take the place of the present United Nations Organization Assembly and Council.

VIII. BUT WE WOULD STILL HAVE COUNTRIES OF OUR OWN

BEFORE we go any further one point should be made very, very clear. A superficial reading of our plan thus far might give the impression that it proposes that, in our new World-State, all present nations will, as such, cease to exist. This is absolutely *not* the fact. It would almost surely be impossible to secure the present acceptance of a new world-state organization, by the people of *any* country, if it were to be the fact. Quite aside, however, from this very practical question of initial acceptance, it is almost surely desirable, in fact highly desirable, that each country continue to go on, as a national entity, very much as it has in the past. Most of us do not believe, as some advocates of a World-State have contended, that the concept of nationality is a wholly evil one. On the contrary, we believe that it has shown, and that it has, enormous capacities for good—and in all sorts of different directions. We believe that for a long interim period at least, national entities will continue to be very important links in the economy and governance of the world.

This plan proposes, therefore, to leave to each nation an unchanged and unquestioned sovereignty over all the *internal* affairs of its own peoples. It may be true, as has indeed been already suggested, that, once we secure a World-State, *political* nationality may prove to be a transitional phase. It may very well be that the complete and immediate breaking up of the *inter-national* functioning of all of the nations will encourage, among their peoples, such a broader view of their internal social and economic problems, that this world view will gradually come to supplant the often narrow, generally dangerously competitive, and sometimes actually chauvinistic, point of view of nationalism. But this elimination of nationalism in all its political aspects is a development that, even if it is desirable, and even if it later comes about, is bound to take time.

So, even politically, nations, as nations, will continue to have their place in the new world order. Even in those countries in which Electoral District boundaries and national boundaries coincide, that is small countries where the District and the Nation cover exactly the same geographical area, the two bodies would be, politically speaking, quite separate and distinct: one would function on behalf of its people's world relationships, the other on behalf of their internal affairs.

My own feeling is that this insistence upon the World-State's non-interference with every nation's *internal* affairs is vitally important. So far as itself is concerned, its own affairs and its own peoples, every nation ought to be left completely alone—to be as wise or as foolish as it pleases! If the Union of Soviet Social Republics wants to continue to operate under its communistic economy, it should be left completely undisturbed to do so. If the United States desires to continue intact its high protective barriers against that larger freedom of trade with the world that it might have, it should continue to have complete power, in its own discretion, to do so. If Great Britain wants to retain its pleasantly anachronistic king, the World-State would not say, or desire to say, a single word to prevent its doing so. In other words, the peoples of each country, no matter how they may vote in the World-State, would continue to run their respective countries exactly as they themselves choose.

Furthermore, they would continue to be held together, as countries, by ties of race and language, by history and precedent, by commonly held customs and a common body of law, by social habits and economic environment. It is only the inter-national implications of nationality that we want to get absolutely away from: everything else about "nationality", its internal political powers, its cultural, linguistic, historical, and sentimental implications are to remain undisturbed. In the new order we shall all become citizens of a World-State—true; but at the same time we shall still continue to be Americans and Britons and Frenchmen and Dutchmen—and proud of it. We shall even be able, if we choose to do so, to do what it is impossible for any of us to do now, i.e. retire into a national isolationism more complete than that of Japan a century ago. There will be, in fact, only one single thing that, as nations, we positively will *not* be permitted to do: we will not be permitted to make war upon our neighbors.

These last paragraphs involve a few sequential ramifications that deserve mention. Because it will be the consistent aim of the World-State to eliminate

every vestige of nationalistic approach to the conduct
of world affairs, the election of World Assembly representatives by World Electoral Districts, instead of
by countries as wholes, was not an accidental device.
It was proposed intentionally as a help in breaking
down nationalism in the conduct of world affairs. It
is true, of course, that, in many of the matters that
would come before the World Assembly, the representatives of the larger countries would tend to vote
as a *bloc;* and nothing would prevent their doing so if
they so wished; but, on many other issues—and probably, over the years, on a gradually increasing number
of issues—they could, and would, split.

Because, as we have already noted, "national interest" is the root-cause of war, and, because the elimination of war from the world is the primary objective
of the World-State, this same "diminishment" of nationalism in all inter-national matters would go much
further than the elimination of national armies and
navies and air powers. Not only would there be, in
this new World-State of ours, none of these, and no
such thing as voters voting for "national" representatives, there would also be no such things as *national*
"foreign offices", or "state departments", or "diplomats", or "consuls". In other words, all present *political* relationships, of every sort whatsoever, between
nations would be immediately abolished; and the
functioning of all the relationships that we have hith-
erto termed "inter-national"* would hereafter be either
centralized in the World-State itself, or decentralized
in its own respective Electoral Districts. It is *they,*

* We have, by the way, no word in the English language to describe
them except "international"!

not the nations, that would have "consuls" and "diplomats" (if there remained need for any such officials). A nation would not only cease to have the means with which to wage war: it would cease to have any machinery of representation with which to argue with other nations about the matters over which a war might be waged. Lacking all of these it would be a little hard to get an inter-national war started. And we need have little fear that the World Electoral District of Connecticut, for example (or that of East Scotland, or that of Marseilles) would attempt to launch a little private war of its own against some other Electoral District. And, if it did try to, with a world police force to crack down on it, it wouldn't be able to get very far.

IX. THE POWERS AND DUTIES OF THE WORLD-STATE

"OH BUT," I can hear someone interrupting at about this point, "your whole thesis, your whole procedural organization, naively assumes a world entirely made up of peoples of good will. It assumes that no monkey-wrenches are going to be thrown into any of your nice machinery. And finally —and this also is an unfounded assumption—it assumes that the only sorts of wars that there are are inter-national ones. It entirely ignores such sad eruptions as civil war and internal revolution and colonial revolt.

"And this last assumption by the way," these critics will continue, "brings up another matter: you say that you are willing to have—in fact that you desire to have—extreme flexibility in the organization of the World-State: but simultaneously you say that you are going in no way whatever to interfere in any nation's own internal affairs. Does not this present an apparent contradiction in the case, for example, of colonial revolt? Do you propose to establish, or at least to encourage, a permanent *status quo* in the make-up of all present colonial possessions?

The answer is "No,"—to every one of these assumptions. And particularly to the last one, delicate as it is, and difficult though it is to answer it categorically. The new World-State will not be set up to freeze any present colonial, or any present national, status. We have said that it would be agreed, at the start, that the World-State would not interfere in any way whatsoever in the internal affairs of any country. And this extreme position would seem to be vitally necessary at the start. It may, in due course, be altered later; but, as we have seen, it will require the almost unanimous consent of all of the countries of the world to effect such an alteration—and this will require a lot of popular education in the meanwhile. But such World-State non-interference in a nation's internal affairs does not mean, necessarily, that changes in colonial status, etc., are going to be rendered impossible. We must remember in the first place that internal revolts and civil wars, in any military sense, are, in our new order, going to be almost impossible to carry on at all, for both sides will lack armament for real war. What such affairs will tend to become, when they do occur, will be disturbances very much like our present strikes, i.e. a combination of economic pressure and what we might term riot violence. It must be admitted that this combination is bad enough, but it surely is not so bad as outright civil war.

Furthermore we may hope that, in a world increasingly familiar with, and addicted to, the ways of peace, internal disputes, when they do arise, may, like international ones, tend to be settled peaceably, and not by force. The World-State will have no power to intervene in any internal issue; but there is another very powerful force that can, and will, intervene— the power of public opinion. The more civilized a state is the more sensitive it is to this force; and, fortunately, our greatest colonial empires are held by our most civilized countries.

We must further remember that oftentimes at present a local disturbance is not really a local affair at all. It is merely a move in a much larger game. A large country sends *agents provacateurs* into a small neighbor country in order to stir up trouble there to serve its own ends, trouble that may be entirely contrary to the wishes of a large majority of the smaller country's inhabitants. This sort of thing the World-State will have every right, and full power, to stop, because it will be a direct interference by one nation in the internal affairs of another nation. In many cases, if there were not this sort of outside exacerbation of a domestic issue, the purely internal differences involved would settle themselves easily by peaceful democratic procedures. On the other hand, there exist now, and there will exist, in some localities genuine deep-seated desire for change of some sort—India is probably a present example. In such cases the attitude of the World-State will have to be one of sympathetic desire to help, not by any display of military force, but by advice and, possibly, by mediation at the request of both parties.

All this brings us back to the question of the exact powers of the World-State. It would seem as though these might have to be on two or three different levels. First, by a simple majority vote, the World Assembly might be empowered to regulate its own elections, and to carry out the duties imposed upon it by its Constitution. By a three-quarters vote, perhaps, it might *approve* recommendations made to it by its cooperating nations, or it might *recommend* to them, changes in that fundamental Constitution. These changes could include such things as: increases in the scope of its own duties (i.e. the giving to it of additional sovereign powers); changes in inter-national boundaries; changes in the internal sovereignty of its member nations (such things as those we have just been talking about, i.e. the setting up of what formerly had been colonies as new independent nations, or the splitting up of present nations into two or more new nations, or even, possibly, combinations of present separate nations into one); changes in its own representational machinery, (i.e. the size of its Assembly, the method of its election, etc.). Finally, and this last perhaps only by a nine-tenths vote of its whole membership, the World-State might put into effect constitutional amendments such as any of these mentioned even though *some* of its constituent national members disapproved of them.

Such a sliding scale of powers as this would ensure that any *one* large power, or a very small group of small powers, would be able to block any changes that they desired to block in the original basic constitution of the World-State. This inflexibility in such an instrument may be criticized. To make any fundamental charter so extremely hard to change may seem unwise: it always, in practice, tends to develop an "unwritten" supplementary "constitution" of procedure and precedent. On the other hand, this extreme resistance to change in the World-State's basic instrument gives very strong assurance indeed to every nation going into it that, in relinquishing its international sovereignty to it, it is not doing something that is making it thereafter helpless: it will always thereafter be able successfully to resist—if it wishes to do so—any *further* invasion whatsoever upon its own sovereign powers. If it be a large power, it can never be forced to give up any more than it has already given up, for even one large power will be able to resist such further invasion. But to the small powers it gives equal assurance; it gives assurance to them that the large powers will not be able, without the almost unanimous approval of the small ones, further to invade *their* sovereignties. Both of these assurances are extremely important. No nation, large or small, when it is asked to join the World-State, wants to do so with the least residuum of feeling that it is sticking its head into a noose which later is going to be drawn tight to strangle it. It wants to know, and to know in advance, exactly how far, without its approval, the World-State will be able to go.

But the duties and powers of this World-State are not problems about which we can give, or need to give, extended attention here. Obviously on them a whole book might easily be written. This slender paper has a different, and very limited, purpose. The main thing to be said here, however, about duties and powers is to repeat what has already been suggested regarding them, viz. that the World-State should, at the start, probably have very few indeed of either. The first, and all-important, of its duties will be the assurance of the world's peace. And, to secure this assurance, the World-State should receive, without any reservation whatsoever, every iota of power that it needs. This means, beyond question, that it alone should control whatever military and naval and air power it is necessary for it to retain for world police purposes. It means also that all such military powers —every single shred of them—would have to be given up, and given up by *every* nation, to the World-State.

But this means, also, in turn, that the World-State must have absolute and unqualified control over the making of all munitions, over the production and use of atomic energy, over the control of such strategic areas as Panama, Gibraltar, Suez, the Dardanelles, and its own headquarters area—wherever the latter may be located. *All* of us would have to give up *all* of these powers *if* we are to have world peace. On this point there can be no compromise. There is no half-way alternative. And that means, equally unqualifiedly, that if, at the start, any nation, or any group of nations, refused to make such an absolutely complete relinquishment of its own military powers to the World-State, the World-State would have to be empowered, and would have to be furnished with the means, to maintain military, naval, aerial and atomic powers of its own overwhelmingly superior, in every respect, to those of that non-cooperating nation, or non-cooperating group of nations. And it would have to continue to maintain these overwhelmingly superior powers for just so long as that nation or group of nations, chose to continue to be militarily non-cooperative. In other words, nothing about this World-State proposal is intended to be quixotic: world peace is never going to be gained by "appeasement," in any form whatsoever. It would be suicidal to make the peace-loving states of the world defenceless against those who refuse to disarm.

But, although world peace would be overwhelmingly the first duty of the new World-State, it would be quite possible, once it had achieved it, for it to go ahead—*if* a substantial majority of its representatives desired it to do so—and gradually take over certain other functions which are now considered to be national. One can envisage, for instance as a *future* possibility, the lowering of the barriers at present hindering world trade. And, by the "lowering of the barriers," we mean such things as world uniformity in the regulation of, and world freedom for, air travel and sea travel, a world-wide system of weights and measures, World-State postal and currency and banking systems, each supplementing, *but not necessarily supplanting,* national postal and currency and banking systems. One can further foresee that, just as the educational standards of all the world ought *ultimately* to be raised to equality—which is going to take time—so ought its economic standards to be. But it cannot be too often repeated that many of these points are extremely nettle-some ones; and that it would surely be well not to attempt to force them, and not to attempt any of them at the start. First things first.

There are one or two further suggestions about the functioning of the Assembly of the World-State that may be worth recording. World Elections might be held only once in each decade. If this were the case, representatives to the World Assembly might better *not* be eligible for reelection. There might be provision that at each election each World Electoral District elect a Representative and an Alternate, the Alternate to have the right to be present, and perhaps even to speak, at meetings of the Assembly, but to have no vote. He would, however, automatically fill the unexpired term of any Representative dying or resigning, and, as he would be eligible for election as a Representative, he could really be an under-study of his Representative. Under this plan a Representative would hold office long enough to become thoroughly familiar with his duties, but would not have to "campaign" for reelection, and would not have the possibility of reelection in mind in any decision he would be called upon to make. The provision for Alternates provides, however, a desirable continuity of policy.

Because, under our plan, new national quotas for Assembly representation would have to be set every ten years, many of the World Electoral District boundaries might, for a long time, be fluid. India, for example, might very well have two Districts in its first election, three or four in its second, and still more in its third. Indeed, we would hope that it would have! In the educationally matured states there would tend to be a corresponding shrinkage in the number of Districts; and these, and internal shifts of population, would tend to cause an equal changeableness in District boundary lines.

It is difficult to over-value the desirability of all of this automatic flexibility in the working organization of the World-State. If we look at this present world of ours with our eyes open it becomes, perhaps disconcertingly, apparent that, quite regardless of the special problems raised by the discovery of atomic energy, no United Nations Organization which has been carefully organized, whether intentionally or not, to maintain the *status quo* is going to work satisfactorily for very long. For a ferment is working in India and in China and in the Moslem world which it would be very unwise indeed for us of the white race to ignore. And it would be an even graver mistake for us to try to keep it under control with battleships and guns. Rather it is for us—who claim to be the more intelligent third of the world's population—to give clear evidence of that intelligence. If we go to these "backward" peoples of the world with schools and hospitals and libraries—and World-State votes—we are going to be welcomed by them with open arms; and we are going to find mutual understanding (and even trade!) inevitably following in the wake of our schools and hospitals.

We are going to ignore at our peril the unescapable fact that, because these peoples are overwhelmingly a majority of the world's population, they are bound —in time—to control it. What kind of a control they are going to exert it is largely for *us* now to decide. Is it not possible, or even probable, that, if we try to establish our new world order on some such an educational basis as the one that has here been suggested, the world will witness a second Revival of Learning, and this time one on a world-wide scale? Can we not foresee a vast demand upon us of the white race, not so much for teachers, as for teachers to teach teachers, and for teachers to teach teachers to teach teachers? Can we not also see education itself raised to a new social importance, to the importance which it has always deserved in the body politic, but which it has received only at long separated intervals in human history?

And, finally, can we not also, under this plan, see every nation's educational progress becoming its primary *patriotic* duty? Instead of "armament races" between nations, can we not envisage educational ones? Instead of a competition between them in pouring out money for bombs and battleships, can we not foresee a *competition* between them in pouring out money for hospitals and libraries and schools? And the splendid thing about *this* sort of inter-national competition is that every indirect result of it would also be socially desirable; for more education always results in a higher standard of living, in more economic security, in less disease, in more religious tolerance, in greater inter-racial understanding, in a wider growth of all the arts. It means, in short, it would seem, the bringing in of the climate, and of the only sort of climate, in which any World-State is ever going to be able to function successfully.

Finally, the writer has no thought that this little book presents in any sense a definitive plan. All that he hopes for it is that it may possibly make a suggestive contribution, provide a slender new clue through a very tangled maze. If it does this it may perhaps supply a tentative start from which others may develop something practically constructive.

Date Due